Date: 4/26/17

J BIO GARCIA
Juarez, Christine,
Hector P. Garcia /

GREAT HISPANIC AND LATINO AMERICANS

Hector P. Garcia

by Christine Juarez

CAPSTONE PRESS
a capstone imprint

Pebble Books are published by Capstone Press,
1710 Roe Crest Drive, North Mankato, Minnesota 56003
www.mycapstone.com

Library of Congress Cataloging-in-Publication Data
Names: Juarez, Christine, 1976–
Title: Hector P. Garcia / by Christine Juarez.
Description: North Mankato, Minnesota : Capstone Press, 2017. | Series: Pebble
books. Great Hispanic and Latino Americans | Audience: K to grade 3. |
Includes bibliographical references and index. Identifiers: LCCN 2016003661 |
ISBN 9781515718918 (library binding) | ISBN 9781515719021 (paperback) | ISBN
9781515719229 (eBook pdf) Subjects: LCSH: Garcia, Hector P., 1914–1996—Juvenile
literature. | Mexican Americans—Biography—Juvenile literature. | Civil rights
workers—United States—Biography—Juvenile literature. | Mexican Americans—
Civil rights—History–20th century—Juvenile literature. | American G.I.
Forum—Juvenile literature. | Physicians—Texas—Biography—Juvenile literature.
Classification: LCC E184.M5 J83 2017 | DDC 973/.0468720092—dc23
LC record available at http://lccn.loc.gov/201600366

Note to Parents and Teachers

The Great Hispanic and Latino Americans series supports national
curriculum standards for social studies related to people, places,
and culture. This book describes and illustrates Hector P. Garcia.
The images support early readers in understanding the text. The
repetition of words and phrases helps early readers learn new
words. This book also introduces early readers to subject-specific
vocabulary words, which are defined in the Glossary section. Early
readers may need assistance to read some words and to use the
Table of Contents, Glossary, Read More, Internet Sites, and Index
sections of the book.

Printed in the United States of America in North Mankato, Minnesota.
009663F16

Table of Contents

1914
born

About Hector

Hector P. Garcia was

a civil rights leader.

He worked for the fair treatment

of all Mexican-Americans.

He was born in Mexico

on January 17, 1914.

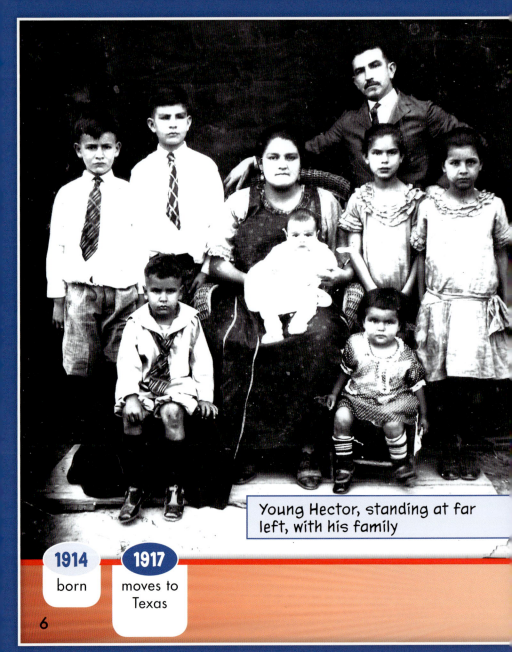

Young Hector, standing at far left, with his family

1914
born

1917
moves to Texas

6

In 1917 Mexico was at war.

Hector's parents wanted

a better life for their children.

That year, the family moved

to the U.S. state of Texas.

1914 born

1917 moves to Texas

1940 graduates from medical school

Hector's parents were teachers.

They wanted their children

to go to college.

In 1940 Hector graduated

from medical school in

Galveston, Texas.

| 1914 | 1917 | 1940 | 1945 |
| born | moves to Texas | graduates from medical school | marries Wanda Fusillo |

Adulthood

Hector served in the U.S. Army during World War II (1939–1945). During the war, he met Wanda Fusillo. They married in 1945. The couple had four children.

1914
born

1917
moves to
Texas

1940
graduates
from medical
school

1945
marries
Wanda
Fusillo

12

After the war, Hector was
a doctor in Texas. He spoke
out for other Mexican-Americans
who had served in the war.
He said these veterans were
not being treated the same
as white veterans.

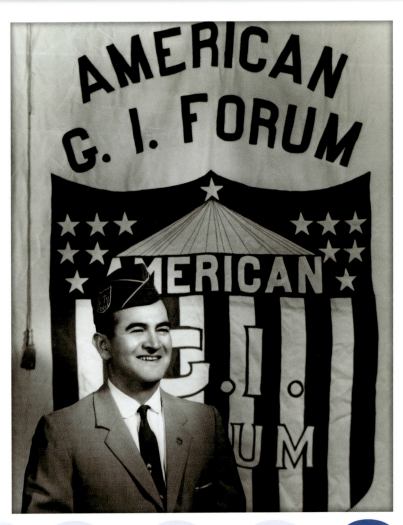

1914	1917	1940	1945	1948
born	moves to Texas	graduates from medical school	marries Wanda Fusillo	forms American G.I. Forum

Working for Equal Rights

In 1948 Hector formed the American G.I. Forum to organize Mexican-American veterans. Together they demanded health and education benefits.

1914	1917	1940	1945	1948
born	moves to Texas	graduates from medical school	marries Wanda Fusillo	forms American G.I. Forum

Through the American G.I. Forum,

Hector improved the lives of

all Mexican-Americans.

Hector worked for equal schools,

health care, jobs, and homes.

President Lyndon Johnson with Hector

1914	1917	1940	1945	1948
born	moves to Texas	graduates from medical school	marries Wanda Fusillo	forms American G.I. Forum

Hector wanted Hispanics to have

a stronger say in government.

In 1961 Hector worked with

President John F. Kennedy.

Then in 1968 President

Lyndon Johnson named him

to a U.S. civil rights group.

1961
works with
President
Kennedy

1968
is named
to U.S. civil
rights group

1914	1917	1940	1945	1948
born	moves to Texas	graduates from medical school	marries Wanda Fusillo	forms American G.I. Forum

Later Years

Hector was the first Mexican-American given the U.S. Medal of Freedom. He received this important honor in 1984. Hector died July 26, 1996. The people of Texas celebrate Hector P. Garcia Day every September.

1961	1968	1984	1996
works with President Kennedy	is named to U.S. civil rights group	receives U.S. Medal of Freedom	dies

Glossary

benefit—money or services given to workers, including military members, in addition to their pay

civil rights—the rights that all people have to freedom and equal treatment under the law

demand—to strongly ask for or request something

forum—the public discussion of an issue

Hispanic—a person of Mexican, South American, or other Spanish-speaking background

veteran—someone who has served in the armed forces

World War II—a war in which the United States, France, Great Britain, the Soviet Union and other countries defeat Germany, Italy, and Japan; World War II lasted from 1939 to 1945

Read More

Arkham, Thomas. *Latino American Civil Rights*. Hispanic Americans: Major Minority. Broomall, Penn.: Mason Crest, 2013.

Ollhoff, Jim. *Identity and Civil Rights*. Hispanic American History. Edina, Minn.: ABDO Pub. Co., 2012.

Internet Sites

FactHound offers a safe, fun way to find Internet sites related to this book. All of the sites on FactHound have been researched by our staff.

Here's all you do:

Visit *www.facthound.com*

Type in this code: 9781515718918

Super-cool stuff! Check out projects, games and lots more at **www.capstonekids.com**

Index

Editorial Credits
Erika L. Shores, editor; Charmaine Whitman, designer;
Kelly Garvin, media researcher; Tori Abraham, production specialist

Photo Credits
Dr. Hector P. Garcia Papers, Mary and Jeff Bell Library Special Collections and
Archives, Texas A&M University-Corpus Christi, cover, 1, 6, 8, 10, 14, 16, 18, 20;
Getty/Steve Larson/The Denver Post, 4; Newscom/Everett Collection, 12
Artistic Elements: Shutterstock: Eliks, nalinn, tuulijumala